Mini Microbes

By Michael Sandler

Scott Foresman
is an imprint of

Glenview, Illinois • Boston, Massachusetts • Chandler, Arizona •
Upper Saddle River, New Jersey

Photographs
Every effort has been made to secure permission and provide appropriate credit for photographic material. The publisher deeply regrets any omission and pledges to correct errors called to its attention in subsequent editions.

Unless otherwise acknowledged, all photographs are the property of Pearson Education, Inc.

Photo locators denoted as follows: Top (T), Center (C), Bottom (B), Left (L), Right (R), Background (Bkgd)

Opener Visuals Unlimited/Corbis; **1** Dave King/©DK Images; **3** ©Dr. Ken MacDonald/ Photo Researchers, Inc.; **4** Visuals Unlimited/Corbis; **6** (BR) ©Westend61 GmbH/Alamy, (BL) Getty Images; **7** (BL) ©Westend61 GmbH/Alamy, (BR) Peter Arnold/Peter Arnold, Inc.; **8** ©SoFood/Alamy, (BR) Dave King/©DK Images; **9** (BR) Oote Boe Photography / Alamy Images; **10** David Murray/©DK Images, (TL) Ian O'Leary/©DK Images, (TR) Maximilian Stock Ltd/Corbis; **11** (TR) David Murray/©DK Images; **12** Jose Luis Pelaez, Inc./Corbis; **13** (B) Keith Morris/Alamy Images; **14** Remi Benali/Corbis; **15** Lester Lefkowitz/Corbis.

ISBN 13: 978-0-328-51658-2
ISBN 10   0-328-51658-9

2 3 4 5 6 7 8 9 10 V054 13 12 11 10

Microbes can live at the very bottom of the ocean.

Microbes are tiny living things. The name microbe comes from two Greek words: *micro*, which means "small," and *bios*, which means "life." Microbes are really, really small forms of life.

Microbes are found everywhere on Earth. They're in the air, in the soil, in lakes and ponds, and even at the bottom of the sea. Even our bodies are filled with microbes. Although the **precise** number can't be counted, scientists think humans may have more than a quadrillion microbes living inside them.

For something so small, microbes can cause big changes. They can help make food that people love, or they can cause food to spoil and rot. Microbes can turn a pile of leaves into a pile of soil. In lakes and oceans, microbes can produce food for other creatures. They also produce much of the oxygen in Earth's atmosphere.

Say the word *microbe,* and some people think of germs. Despite some people's fears, most germs don't actually make people sick.

An **analysis** of microbes shows that most microbes are much more helpful and much less harmful than people think.

Microbes seen through a microscope

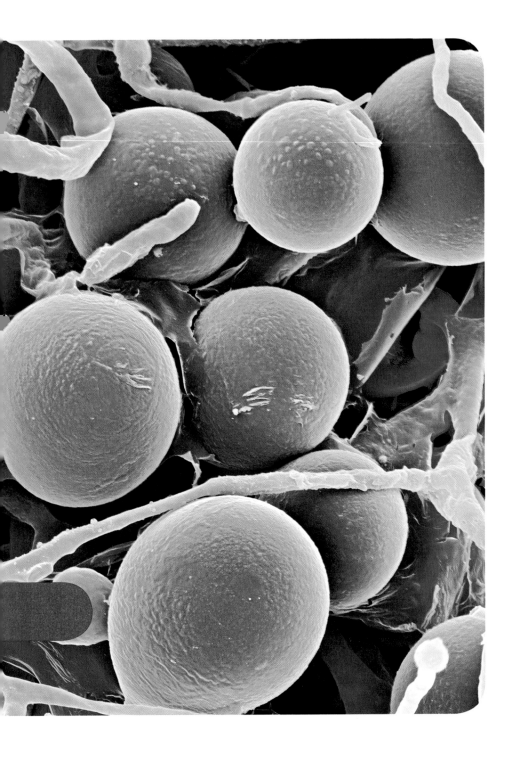

Microbes can't be seen without a **microscope**. However we don't need **beakers** and microscopes to see the remarkable changes microbes can cause.

Here's an experiment. Take a slice of bread and place it on a plate. Leave it out in the open air.

Check the slice of bread every day. After a day or two, you may begin to see something new. The bread will have some blue-green or

Mold will grow on a slice of bread under the right conditions.

gray spots or fuzz. Those are microbes called mold. Where did they come from? The air. There are all kinds of microbes in the air, even if you can't see them.

If the bread is left out for several weeks, it becomes moldier until it's entirely covered. Eventually, the bread will fall apart. Microbes are feeding on the bread and reproducing so that there are more and more of them. That is how a small spot of mold can grow into a fuzzy blanket.

Moldy bread doesn't sound good to eat. However, many foods that people love are created with the help of microbes.

Bread is a perfect example. Yeast is a microbe that is used to make bread rise. If yeast didn't exist, then breakfast toast would be as flat as the flattest pancake. *Why?* you may ask.

Yeast microbes cause bread to rise.

Bread dough is generally made from flour, sugar, and water. When yeast is added to the mixture, it feeds on the sugar that is in the dough. Yeast microbes are **relentless** eaters. As they eat, they create gas bubbles. Like bubbles in a glass of soda, the gas bubbles made by the yeast rise. They push up and lift the dough and create little **hollow** spaces and tiny holes. Now the bread dough is ready for baking!

Microbes are responsible for many of the foods we eat.

Not all microbes act in the same way. One set of microbes can make a container of milk turn sour. However, put a different set of microbes into the same milk, and you get creamy cottage cheese.

If just the right microbes are added to brine in a jar, they can slowly turn crunchy cucumbers into tasty pickles. Other microbes turn milk into

yogurt. Still others can turn apple juice into a bubbly cider.

How do they do it? The microbes eat and reproduce, creating more and more microbes. At the same time, they also excrete, or give off, waste products. These waste products make bubbles in dough or slime on a banana.

The tiny living things people call "germs" are also microbes. Most people think all germs will make them sick. In fact, most don't. The human body has many ways to fight harmful microbes and keep us healthy.

Washing hands removes microbes that could make you sick.

Still, it is a good idea to avoid such germs. Every time someone sneezes or coughs, germs fly into the air. Every time someone touches a doorknob, they are touching germs. That's why people **lecture** about the need to wash hands and clean fruits and vegetables to remove germs.

When germs make us sick, we must wait for our bodies to fight off the infection. We may also need to take medicines such as penicillin to help us feel better.

Amazingly, penicillin is actually made from microbes! In 1928 scientist Alexander Fleming discovered that something was wrong with one of his experiments. It didn't take him long to **identify** the problem. It was mold. That mold, he discovered, could be used to make penicillin, which, in turn, could kill other microbes that caused disease.

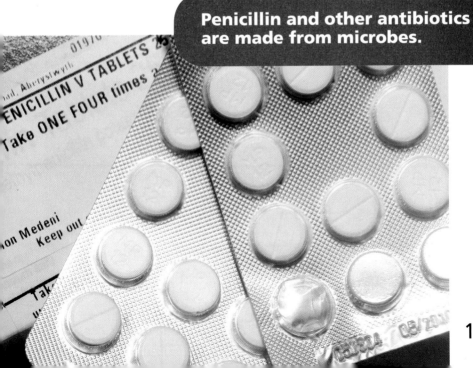

Penicillin and other antibiotics are made from microbes.

Microbes can also help clean up the environment. Scientists have known for a long time that certain microbes eat oil. Recently, scientists have begun to use microbes to clean up oil spills.

In an oil spill, oil coats the water, animals, plants —everything. The trick is to get rid of the oil quickly and safely. Scientists are learning how to add microbes and specific chemicals to the water. Those chemicals help the microbes eat and reproduce faster to better remove the oil.

Special microbes are used in oil spills to remove the oil.

We couldn't live without microbes.

Microbes help the environment in other ways. Microbes are always hungry. Microbes can be found on the ground and underground. There, along with insects and animals, they eat. They help break apart dead plant and animal material. They help these things decompose and allow nutrients to go back into the soil.

Too small to be seen, microbes all around us have some big effects on the world. Microbes are everywhere, and we couldn't live without them.

Glossary

analysis *n.* a method of studying a thing or determining its essential features

beakers *n.* thin, flat-bottomed glass cups with no handles, used in laboratories

hollow *adj.* having nothing inside

identify *v.* recognize

lectures *n.* a planned speech or talk, usually for the purpose of instruction

microscopes *n.* a tool with lenses for magnifying very small things

precise *adj.* very exact or accurate

relentless *adj.* without pity; harsh